Craft the Perfect *frame*

Craft the Perfect *frame*

Transform Plain Frames with Papers, Paints, and Embellishments

Carin Heiden Atkins

Creative Publishing
international

Chanhassen, Minnesota

Copyright 2006
Creative Publishing international
18705 Lake Drive East
Chanhassen, Minnesota 55317
1-800-328-3895
www.creativepub.com
All rights reserved

**Creative Publishing
international**

President/CEO: Ken Fund
Vice President/Publisher: Linda Ball
Vice President/Retail Sales: Kevin Haas

Executive Editor: Alison Brown Cerier
Senior Editor: Linda Neubauer
Stylist: Joanne Wawra
Art Directors: Brad Springer, Tim Himsel
Photographer: Andrea Rugg
Production Manager: Laura Hokkanen

Illustrator: M. Deborah Pierce
Cover Design: Rule 29
Page Design and Layout: Michaelis Carpelis Design

Library of Congress Cataloging-in-Publication Data

Atkins, Carin Heiden, 1973-
  Craft the perfect frame : transform plain frames with papers, paints,
and embellishments / by Carin Heiden Atkins.
      p. cm.
  ISBN 1-58923-209-7 (soft cover)
  1. Picture frames and framing. 2. Decoration and ornament. I. Title.

TT899.2.A85 2005
749'.7--dc22

                              2005010606

Printed in China:
10 9 8 7 6 5 4 3 2 1

About the Author

Carin Heiden Atkins is a designer, author, and speaker for the craft industry. Her expertise encompasses home accessories design, paper crafting, scrapbooking, calligraphy, floral design, interior decorating, decorative painting, and general crafting. Carin is the author of *Elegant Porcelain and Glass Painting Projects*.

Acknowledgments

This book wouldn't have been possible without the wonderful team of people at Creative Publishing international. You all have my eternal gratitude for putting so much energy and passion into this project.

Thanks to my husband, David, whose support and love have been so appreciated during this project and always.

Thank you to my grandmother, Sylvia Lock, and my mother, Drinda Heiden, for being a tremendous resource for the photos I used in the frames in this book.

Thank you to my friends Tera, Jane, Kirsten, Trish, and Valerie for your support and friendship. I appreciate each of you more than you know!

This book would not have been possible without the products and support of the following manufacturers: Anna Griffin (Anna and Tracey), Delta (Tiffany and Kim), K&Company (Holly and Therese), Loew-Cornell (Shirley), Making Memories (Kelly, Jen, and Andrew), Midori Ribbon (Midori and Baydra), Pebeo (Angela and Yves), Ranger Inc (Anne, Robin, and Tera), and Walnut Hollow (Chris).

Contents

Getting Started

Victorian Roses and Butterflies, the frame shown on the cover of this book, holds a photograph of my great-grandparents as a young couple. I love this family heirloom and wanted to display it in an elegant setting reminiscent of their era. I bought a frame and mat, then added richness and color with gorgeous papers. I added some drama and dimension with die cuts of roses and butterflies, raised above the surface. Now the frame hangs in my home, where we enjoy it every day.

You, too, can showcase your favorite photographs, artwork, and decorative objects. *Craft the Perfect Frame* has been created to provide techniques and inspiration for transforming plain frames. Creating these frames has been a labor of love, and each of them has special meaning to me. I hope that they will inspire you to craft your own perfect frames!

Each project starts with a purchased frame (no need to get out the miter box and construct it). The frame or mat is then dressed up with a variety of sensational papers, paints, and embellishments. If you already enjoy making scrapbooks, many of the products and techniques will be familiar to you. Don't worry, though, if you have never set foot in a scrapbook store, because all of the projects are easy enough for general crafters of any skill level.

If you want to use the same papers and decorative materials as I did, the source list on page 112 will help you find them. I encourage you to add or subtract elements of my designs as you like, or to use the techniques with different materials or in your own ways.

Before you begin, please read through this helpful overview of the materials you'll be using. You won't need all the materials for every project, but this will help you see the possibilities.

What to Frame

Photographs are the most commonly framed objects. Photos bring back memories, and they speak to our hearts. Every photo tells a story. We honor and remember the people we love by framing their pictures and placing them in our homes. We surround ourselves with photographs of weddings, babies, and vacations. If you are a scrapbooker, you already know the pleasure of putting a photo in a perfect setting. These projects are the perfect extension of scrapbooking. Take your projects out of the book and onto the wall, where everyone can see them!

Think outside the photo box, too. Frame a work of art or a craft project, whether it is by an artist or by a child. You can also frame memorabilia and decorative objects. I found artistic ways to display the seashells from a beach vacation and the wine corks saved from special occasions. One of my favorite framed pieces features a place setting of silverware. Look around your home for family heirlooms, medals, or jewelry. Even silk flowers from the craft store can become dramatic artwork for your home.

The Frames

In designing the projects for this book, I started with a variety of purchased frames.

Unfinished wood craft frames, square or shaped, can be painted in many ways, covered with paper, or covered with self-adhesive fabric. Standard wood and metal frames come with glass and backing boards, and many also have precut mat boards.

Scrapbook frames are designed to hold a 12" (30.5 cm) square scrapbook page and have extra depth to accommodate the thickness of layered papers and notions. Also available in double size, 12" × 24" (30.5 × 61 cm), they come with glass and a backing board.

Shadow boxes consist of a frame and glass fitted over a box for displaying items or collections that have too much depth for a normal frame. Some shadow boxes come with a precut mat at the front, creating a "window well" for showcasing decorative items.

Document frames, intended to hold certificates or diplomas, are made of two pieces of glass (or Plexiglas®) held together in a slim metal frame. Inexpensive ones are simply a piece of glass and a backing board held together with metal clips. Either style can be painted in unique ways.

Mini frames are available in lots of styles, all just waiting for a creative hand to make them really special.

Mats

The mat boards cut for the projects in this book are covered with decorative papers, so there is no need for a special mat cutter to cut a beveled edge and no need to worry about over-cutting corners. All you need is a craft knife, cutting mat, and metal ruler. In some projects, the photo is mounted on top of the mat. When the project requires a mat board with beveled edges, it is already a part of the purchased frame or can be bought separately in a standard size. For several projects, I have used foam core board for the mounting board. Besides adding depth, foam core is wonderfully lightweight and easy to cut.

Materials and Tools

The materials used in the projects are readily available in craft, fabric, or scrapbook stores. Most of the papers are 12" (30.5 cm) square, designed for standard scrapbook pages. A few projects call for art papers that are sold in larger sizes. Though I have been specific about the designs and colors of papers, feel free to select papers that suit your taste and décor.

Papers can be cut with scissors or a craft knife, cutting mat, and metal ruler. Another handy tool is a personal paper trimmer that has a built-in ruler for measuring and a sharp concealed blade for smooth and even cutting. Most trimmers accommodate the full 12" (30.5 cm) width of scrapbook papers. Paper edges are often trimmed with decorative-edge scissors, available in several styles including zigzags and tiny scallops. You will want to use small scissors with sharp points for the more intricate work. Two projects require a circle cutter, which is a handy tool for any crafter to have for cutting circles of all sizes.

Various glues and adhesives are used throughout the book, including hot glue, spray adhesive, fabric glue, and rubber cement. I often use clear double-stick tape for adhering two items to each other. Pop-up dots, used to create space between the two items being joined, have adhesive on both sides. Look for these and other handy products at a paper-crafting store or in the paper-crafting department of a craft store.

Craft paints are available in many forms. Some are perfect for painting on wood while others are made for glass. Dimensional paints that come in tubes have opened up new decorative possibilities. All the paints recommended for the projects are water-based for easy cleanup.

Simple Elegance

Layering papers

An elegant frame doesn't have to be complicated. With easy paper crafting, you can create an attractive setting for any photograph. This frame has a backing board that swings open and holds a sheet of scrapbook paper for the background. Extra depth between the glass and backing board allows you to add dimensional elements. I chose papers that reflect the decorating style of the era in which this wedding photo was taken.

MATERIALS

- ✦ 12" (30.5 cm) square gold scrapbooking frame
- ✦ Rubber cement
- ✦ 12" (30.5 cm) square paper, one sheet each of yellow damask scroll; sage green tweed pattern; blue damask scroll; straw tweed pattern; and pink bouquets, scrolls, and doves
- ✦ Bone folder
- ✦ Paper trimmer
- ✦ Pinking decorative-edge scissors
- ✦ Sharp-tip scissors
- ✦ Foam core board, ¼" (6 mm) thick
- ✦ Craft knife and cutting mat
- ✦ Metal ruler
- ✦ Pencil
- ✦ Double-stick tape
- ✦ Small hole punch
- ✦ Four decorative brads

1. Open the frame back and brush an even coat of rubber cement on the backing board. Position yellow damask scroll paper and smooth it into place with the bone folder.

2. Cut a 10½" (26.7 cm) square of sage green tweed paper, using the paper trimmer. Adhere it to the center of the yellow damask scroll paper, using rubber cement.

3. Cut a 10" (25.5 cm) square of blue damask scroll paper; trim the edges with the pinking decorative-edge scissors. Adhere it to the center of the sage tweed paper, using rubber cement.

4. Cut four strips of straw tweed paper 11 × ¾" (28 × 2 cm). Cut a V-notch in each end of each strip. Set the strips aside.

5. Cut an 8¼" (21.2 cm) square of foam core board for an inner frame, using the craft knife, cutting board, and metal ruler. Cut an opening in the center ½" (1.3 cm) smaller in both directions than the photo that will be framed.

6. Apply an even coat of rubber cement to the front of the foam core frame. Place the frame facedown on the back of the pink bouquet paper. Trace the frame opening onto the paper. Mark an X from corner to corner in the traced opening. Using a craft knife, cut the X, creating four flaps. Cut the flaps to within 1" (2.5 cm) of the marked opening.

7. Apply double-stick tape to the inner edge of each flap. Turn the flaps inward and secure them to the back of the foam core frame. To secure the outer edges, first fold the corners in diagonally and secure with small pieces of double-stick tape. Then apply double-stick tape to the four edges, turn them inward, and secure them to the frame back.

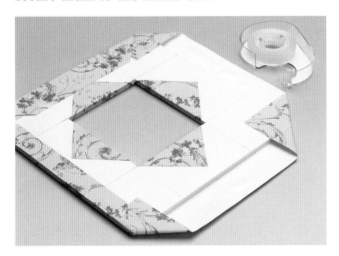

8. Apply double-stick tape to the back edges of the foam core frame. Adhere the straw tweed strips to the frame sides, allowing half of the strip to show from the front. Punch a hole in each corner of the overlapping strips and attach a decorative brad.

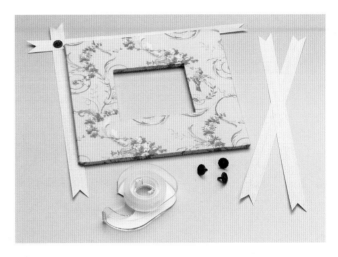

9. Attach your photograph to the back of the foam core frame. Apply two lines of double-stick tape on each side of the back of the foam core frame. Secure it to the center of the blue damask scroll paper.

10. Reassemble the frame.

Dressed in Pink

Scalloped frames with paper medallions

Two-sided papers make it easy to coordinate patterns and colors. I just couldn't resist playing with this paper in the chic color scheme of pink and brown. A small, scalloped wood frame makes a playful setting for photographs of children or pets. Stacked paper circles cut with decorative-edge scissors form the medallions that accent the four corners of the picture.

MATERIALS

◆ Scalloped-edge wood craft frame

◆ 12" (30.5 cm) square double-sided paper: two sheets downtown dot/solid pink, one sheet bias cut skirt/solid brown, one sheet petite paisley, and one sheet solid light pink

◆ Pencil

◆ Sharp-tip scissors

◆ Metal ruler

◆ Craft knife and cutting mat

◆ Rubber cement

◆ Paper trimmer

◆ Decorative-edge scissors: mini pinking, peaks, and mini scallop

◆ Circle cutter or compass and scissors

◆ Four decorative brads

◆ Thick rubber band

1. Lay the frame facedown on the solid pink side of the downtown dot paper close to a corner. Trace the outline of the frame carefully onto the paper, including the picture window. Set the frame aside and cut out the shape, cutting just inside the outer lines. Using a pencil and metal ruler, mark an X from corner to corner in the picture window. Measure the thickness of the frame and draw another square inside the first one this distance away. Cut out the smaller square, and then cut diagonally into the corners of the larger square, using the craft knife, cutting mat, and metal ruler.

2. Apply a thick coat of rubber cement to the front of the wood frame and the sides of the picture window. Allow the rubber cement to tack up for a minute or two. Adhere the paper cutout to the frame front and smooth the inner edges onto the sides of the picture window.

3. Using the paper trimmer, cut four 12" (30.5 cm) strips of solid pink paper the same width as the frame thickness. Set them aside to be used in step 8. Cut five strips of solid pink paper ½" × 7" (1.3 × 18 cm), and four strips of bias cut skirt paper ⅝" × 7" (1.5 × 18 cm). Edge the solid pink paper strips on both sides with the mini pinking decorative-edge scissors.

4. Apply rubber cement to the backs of the four short, solid pink paper strips and adhere them to the center of the bias cut stripe paper strips. Cut a V-notch at each end of each strip.

5. Apply rubber cement to the back of each layered strip. Adhere them to the frame front ¼" (6 mm) from the opening, forming a border.

6. Cut four 1½" (3.8 cm) circles of brown paper (the reverse side of the bias cut stripe paper), using the circle cutter. Edge the circles with mini pinking decorative-edge scissors. Using sharp-tip scissors, snip little slits in the circle at the notches in the pinked edge, creating fringe. Cut four 1⅜" (3.5 cm) circles of solid pink paper. Edge the pink circles with peaks decorative-edge scissors. Cut four 1" (2.5 cm) petite paisley circles. Cut four ¾" (2 cm) solid light pink circles. Edge the small light pink circles with mini scalloped decorative-edge scissors. To make each medallion, glue four circles together from smallest to largest. Poke a hole in the center of the layered circles and attach a decorative brad.

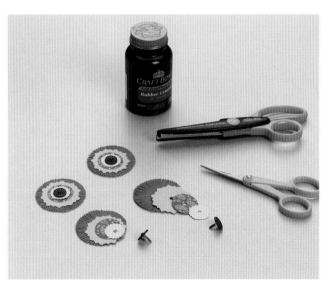

7. Glue three medallions over the border intersections, starting in the upper left corner and working clockwise. Cut the remaining solid pink strip of paper into three pieces. Cut a V-notch in each end of each strip. Glue the strips to the back of the medallion, crisscrossing each other. Glue the last medallion over the intersection in the lower left corner.

8. Adhere the solid pink strips (from step 3) to the frame edge, using rubber cement. Butt strips together tightly where they meet. A rubber band stretched around the outside of the frame will help hold the pieces in place until the rubber cement dries.

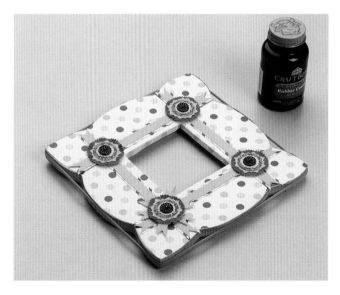

Love Songs

Calligraphy mat

To set a sentimental tone for this photograph, I penned the titles of love songs onto the mat. You can write anything you like, to reflect the mood of your photograph. It is wise to practice on a plain piece of paper first to see how the words will fit on the mat. If you are not a confident calligrapher, write the words in your own hand-writing or use rub-on letters and words or stickers that express your thoughts.

MATERIALS

+ Frame with mat

+ Spray adhesive for fabric

+ Lightweight fabric in desired color

+ Black and white photograph, 1" (2.5 cm) smaller than mat opening

+ Calligraphy pen or fine-tip marker with black ink

+ Stickers or rub-ons (letters or words), optional

+ A list of favorite song titles or favorite quotes

+ Acid-free double-stick tape or adhesive dots

1. Remove the backing board and mat from the frame. Spray the backing board, using spray adhesive. Adhere the fabric to the backing board, and trim the fabric even with the edges of the backing board.

2. Using calligraphy or your best handwriting, write song titles or famous quotes within the area of the mat that will be showing when the frame is assembled. Alternatively, apply stickers (opposite, top) or rub-on words (opposite, bottom) to the mat.

3. Place the mat over the backing board. Place double-stick tape or adhesive dots on the back corners of your photograph, and adhere the photo in the center of the opening.

4. Reassemble the frame.

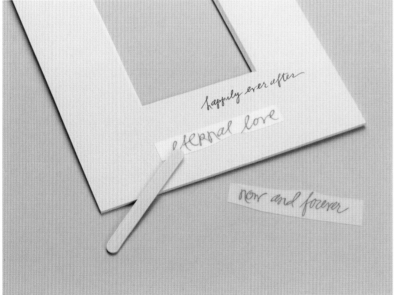

DESIGNER'S TIP

Another way to transfer sentiments to the mat is to decoupage torn pieces of sheet music for your favorite love song, following step 8 on page 27.

Vintage Paris

Collage of maps and postcard papers

Beautiful art paper depicting vintage postcards of Paris inspired me to create this frame. I decoupaged torn pieces of the postcard paper onto the inner mat. The outer mat is covered with an art paper map of Paris. Narrow bands of green paper run through a crimper provide a textured border around the inner mat. Choose similar papers that spotlight your favorite vacation spots, to make your own framed artwork.

MATERIALS

- ◆ Gold frame with mat
- ◆ Art paper, one sheet each of Paris map, green Florentine, and Paris vintage postcard
- ◆ Scissors
- ◆ Rubber cement
- ◆ Craft knife and cutting mat
- ◆ Metal ruler
- ◆ Paper crimper
- ◆ Small hole punch
- ◆ Gold paint pen
- ◆ Four decorative brads
- ◆ Mat board
- ◆ Soft-bristle wash brush, 1" (2.5 cm) wide
- ◆ Decoupage medium

1. Remove the mat and backing board from the frame.

2. Cut the Paris map art paper to match the four sides of the mat, using scissors. Cut the ends of the side pieces diagonally to form mitered corners. Adhere the top and bottom strips in place, using rubber cement. Adhere the side strips in place.

3. Cut five strips of Florentine paper ½" (1.3 cm) wide, using the craft knife, cutting mat, and metal ruler. Run each strip through the paper crimper. Lay four of the pieces out on the mat ¼" (6 mm) from the opening to create a border. Punch a small hole in each corner where they intersect. Cut a V-notch in each end of each strip, just short of the outer edge of the mat.

4. Cut eight 2" (5 cm) pieces from the remaining crimped paper. Cut a V-notch in each end of each strip. Punch a small hole in the center of each piece.

5. Gild the heads of the decorative brads, using the gold paint pen. Allow the brads to dry.

6. Cross two of the short crimped pieces and lay them over an intersection of the mat border, aligning the holes. Insert a decorative brad through the holes to secure the strips together, arranging the short pieces in an X-shape. Repeat at each corner. Adhere the crimped paper border in place, using rubber cement.

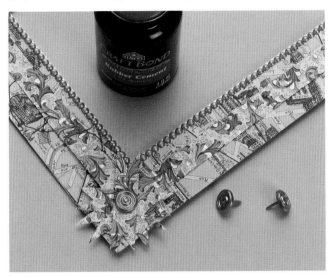

7. Cut a second mat with the outer measurements the same size as the original mat and opening suitable for the picture you intend to use.

8. Rip the postcard paper into pieces of different sizes. Arrange the pieces on the inner mat, overlapping them as necessary. Adhere the pieces to the mat, using the decoupage medium. Brush on a top coat of decoupage medium over the mat. Allow the decoupage medium to dry thoroughly.

9. Mount the photograph behind the inner mat. Reassemble the frame.

Victorian Roses and Butterflies

Paper pleating and pop-ups

Background papers with patterns and colors reminiscent of an elegant past create just the right setting for this photograph of my great-grandparents. Die-cut paper roses and butterflies give the frame dimension and drama. Pop-up adhesive dots add space between the layers. One sheet of scrapbooking paper fits exactly on the backing board of this scrapbook frame. The pleated green border adds even more dimension.

- 12" (30.5 cm) square gold frame
- Spray adhesive
- 12" (30.5 cm) square paper, one sheet each of red damask scrolls, yellow damask scrolls, green-on-green paisley, and brown scroll stripe
- Bone folder
- Foam core board, 1/8" (3 mm) thick
- Craft knife and cutting mat
- Metal ruler
- Pencil
- Double-stick tape
- Paper trimmer
- Sharp-tip scissors
- Six sheets cream rose die cuts
- Four sheets butterfly die cuts
- Pop-up adhesive dots

1. Open the frame back. Apply spray adhesive to the inside of the backing board. Adhere the red floral paper to the backing board and smooth it in place, using the bone folder.

2. Cut a 7½" × 9" (19.3 × 23 cm) piece of foam core board for an inner frame, using a craft knife, cutting mat, and metal ruler. Cut an opening in the center ½" (1.3 cm) smaller in both directions than the photo that will be used.

3. Spray the front of the foam core frame with spray adhesive. Place the frame facedown on the back of the yellow damask scroll paper. Trim the yellow damask scroll paper to within 1" (2.5 cm) of the edges of the foam core board. Trace the frame opening onto the paper. Mark an X from corner to corner in the traced opening. Using the craft knife, cut the X, creating four flaps. Cut the flaps to within 1" (2.5 cm) of the marked opening.

4. Apply double-stick tape to the inner edge of each flap. Turn the flaps inward and secure them to the back of the foam core frame. To secure the outer edges, first fold the corners in diagonally, and adhere with small pieces of double-stick tape. Apply double-stick tape to the four edges, turn them inward, and adhere them to the frame back (see photo step 7, page 15).

5. Cut eight strips of green-on-green paisley paper, 1" (2.5 cm) wide, using the paper trimmer. Cut the plain ribbon strips from the brown scroll stripe paper; reserve the scroll stripes for another project.

6. Pleat the green paper strips to create borders for the frame, following the diagram. Make two borders for the top and bottom with three stacked box pleats each and two borders for the sides with four stacked box pleats each. Burnish the folds with the bone folder. When it is necessary to join strips, overlap them inconspicuously and secure with double-stick tape.

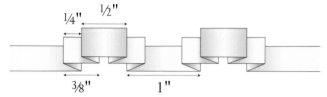

7. Apply double-stick tape to the back edges of the foam core frame. Adhere brown paper strips to the frame sides, allowing ¼" (6 mm) to show from the front. Cut the overlapping corners at 45-degree angles to create mitered corners. Adhere the folded green strips in the same way, allowing them to extend ½" (1.3 cm) beyond the brown strips. Miter the corners.

8. Pop out two cream rose cluster die cuts from the packaging. Trim any paper nubs, using sharp-tip scissors. Using double-stick tape, secure one rose cluster in the upper right corner and one in the lower left corner. Remove two butterfly die cuts from their packaging and trim any paper nubs. Apply double-stick tape to the back of the butterflies and adhere them to top of the rose clusters.

9. Pop out individual flowers from the packaging and trim any paper nubs. Apply a pop-up adhesive dot on one edge of the back of a flower and adhere it on top of the same flower in the rose cluster to create a dimensional effect. Repeat for the other flowers.

10. Pop out the other two butterflies from the packaging and trim any paper nubs. Fold the wings up and apply pop-up adhesive dots under the wings, close to the body. Adhere the butterflies directly on top of the first butterflies. Add more layers of flowers or leaves as desired.

11. Using double-stick tape, adhere your photograph to the back of the foam core frame. Apply double-stick tape to the underside of the foam core frame and attach it in the middle of the red damask scroll paper. Press firmly in place. Reassemble the frame.

Springtime Garden

Layered paper die cuts

Here is a great way to feature two related photos of different sizes. Matching paper borders are cut in different widths. Then the photos are secured to identical mounting boards. The backing board of this frame holds two full sheets of scrapbook paper. Daffodils and hyacinths, cut from more of the same paper, are layered on top with pop-up dots, creating a lively, three-dimensional springtime scene.

- 12" × 24" (30.5 × 61 cm) gold frame
- Spray adhesive
- 12" (30.5 cm) square paper: five sheets daffodil glitter paper, two sheets daffodil plaid paper, two sheets yellow vine flocked paper, and one sheet vine stripe embossed paper
- Two mat boards, 8" × 10" (20.5 × 25.5 cm)
- Rubber cement
- Bone folder
- Paper trimmer
- Decorative-edge scissors: seagull and mini pinking
- Sharp-tip scissors
- Acid-free adhesive dots
- Craft knife and cutting mat
- Pop-up adhesive dots

1. Remove the backing board from the frame. Spray the backing board with spray adhesive. Carefully adhere two sheets of daffodil paper so the center seam is barely visible.

2. Spray the front of an 8" × 10" (20.5 × 25.5 cm) mat board with spray adhesive. Center the board, facedown, on the wrong side of a plaid paper. Apply rubber cement to the remaining paper flaps. Wrap the corners to the back diagonally. Then wrap the sides to the back. Smooth the paper into place with the bone folder. Repeat for the second mat board.

3. Cut eight strips of yellow vine flocked paper 2" (5 cm) wide, using the paper trimmer. Edge one side of each strip with seagull decorative-edge scissors, and set them aside. Cut strips of the vine stripe embossed paper about ¾" (2 cm) wide, centering the yellow vine. Edge one side of each strip with mini pinking decorative-edge scissors. Using sharp-tip scissors, cut snips at each V-notch along the pinked edges, creating fringe. Set the fringed strips aside.

4. Mount a photo in the center of each mat board, using acid-free adhesive dots. Using rubber cement, adhere the yellow vine flocked paper strips around the edge of the photo, mitering the corners. Apply three or four acid-free adhesive dots to the back of each vine embossed strip. Adhere the embossed strips over the flocked strips so they slightly overlap the picture; miter the corners.

5. Apply spray adhesive to the back of each photo board. Press the photo boards in place 3" (7.5 cm) from the sides of the backing board, leaving 3" (7.5 cm) between them.

6. Cut the flowers and bugs from the remaining daffodil paper, using the craft knife and cutting mat. Apply pop-up adhesive dots to the backs of the pieces and secure them over the matching flowers and bugs in the background.

Military Honors

Paper-crafted flag and flourishes

My grandfather's service picture and my father's military school picture just begged to be framed together. Like father, like son. This double scrapbook-page frame with its extra depth allowed me to mount the photos on gold paper-covered boards over a three-dimensional paper flag background. Reinforcing the patriotic theme, red, white, and blue paper strips form borders around the photos.

MATERIALS

- 12" × 24" (30.5 × 61 cm) gold frame
- Large art paper, one sheet each of white, blue, red, and metallic gold
- Spray adhesive
- Metal ruler
- Scissors
- Rubber cement
- Two pieces of mat board, 8" × 10" (20.5 × 25.5 cm)
- Bone folder
- Two photos, 5" × 7" (12.7 × 18 cm)
- Decorative-edge scissors: pinking and mini pinking
- Acid-free adhesive dots
- Paper crimper
- Pencil
- Small hole punch
- Two packages of square decorative brads in antique copper finish
- Embossing stylus

1. Remove the backing board of the frame. Cut the sheet of white art paper to fit the frame backing. Adhere the paper to the front of the backing board with spray adhesive.

2. Place the sheet of blue art paper at an angle over the paper-covered backing in the upper left corner so it extends 7" (18 cm) down the left side, 14" (35.5 cm) across the top, with the lower right corner 2" (5 cm) from the top. Cut out the shape and adhere it to the backing, using rubber cement.

3. Cut 14 strips of red art paper 1¼" × 26" (3.2 × 66 cm). Adhere one strip at an angle, flush with the bottom of the blue paper on the backing board, using rubber cement. Adhere other red strips parallel to the first one, leaving 1" (2.5 cm) spaces between them, until the flag is complete. Trim the ends of the red strips even with the board edge.

4. Cut two pieces of gold art paper 10" × 12" (25.5 × 30.5 cm). Spray the front of an 8" × 10" (20.5 × 25.5 cm) mat board, using spray adhesive. Center the board, sticky side down, on the wrong side of a 10" × 12" (25.5 × 30.5 cm) gold paper. Apply rubber cement to the paper flaps. Wrap the corners to the back diagonally. Then wrap the sides to the back. Smooth the paper into place with the bone folder. Repeat for the second mat board.

5. Cut two pieces of red art paper 6" × 8" (15 × 20.5 cm), using pinking decorative-edge scissors. Apply adhesive dots to the backs of two photographs. Mount the photos to the center of the red art paper. Adhere the mounted photos to the center of the gold boards, using rubber cement.

6. Cut eight ½" (1.3 cm) strips of white art paper. Cut the ends into points, leaving four 10" (25.5 cm) strips and four 8" (20.5 cm) strips. Cut eight ¾" (2 cm) strips of blue art paper, using mini pinking decorative-edge scissors. Run the blue strips through the paper crimper. Cut a V-notch in each end of each strip, leaving four 10" (25.5 cm) strips and four 8" (20.5 cm) strips. Apply rubber cement to the back of each white strip and center the strip over the corresponding crimped blue strip.

7. Arrange the white and blue strips in a border around each photograph. Mark the overlapping corners lightly with a pencil. Punch a hole in the center of each intersection, and secure the strips together with a decorative brad. Adhere the border in place, using rubber cement.

8. Cut 13 stars out of the gold art paper. Turn the stars facedown. Using the embossing stylus, run a line from the tip of each point to the center of the star. Run a second set of lines from the inner corners to the center. Fold the stars wrong sides together on the long lines and right sides together on the short lines to give the stars dimension.

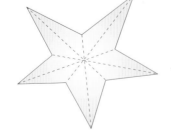

9. Mount the gold picture boards in place with spray adhesive, positioning them about 3" (7.5 cm) from the sides and 3" (7.5 cm) apart.

10. Cut 1¼" (3.2 cm) strips of blue art paper, to create waves in the flag. Beginning at the bottom of the star field, tack one end in place with rubber cement. Form a slight arch in the strip. Trim the strip to the necessary length, and tack down the opposite end, tucking it under the gold photo board. Finish the wave on the other side of the photo board. Repeat with the next row of waves, leaving 1" (2.5 cm) between waves. Repeat with red strips, left over from step 3, securing them over the flat red strips.

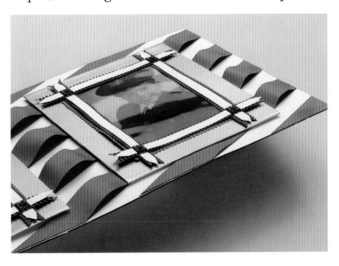

11. Adhere the gold paper stars, using rubber cement.

12. Reassemble the frame.

Paper Roses

Faux mosaic

Now there is a way to create the popular look of mosaic tiles with paper. A friend of mine, Tera Leigh, developed the method and faux mosaic product kit. The result is lighter in weight than real mosaics (great for a picture frame) and doesn't have sharp edges. The technique is easy and fun to do, even for children, and everything cleans up with water. A flat, wood frame makes a great base. Choose any scrapbook paper in a design that suits your photo.

- ✦ Wood craft frame
- ✦ Faux Mosaic Kit™
- ✦ Soft-bristle paintbrush, 1" (2.5 cm) wide
- ✦ 12" (30.5 cm) square paper, one sheet each of pink, tobacco brown, pink and brown stripe, and roses
- ✦ Paper trimmer
- ✦ Sharp-tip scissors
- ✦ Toothpick

1. Apply a thick, even coat of faux grout (step 1 of the Faux Mosaic Kit) to the frame front, sides, and inner edges of the opening, using the soft-bristle paintbrush. Allow the grout to dry completely.

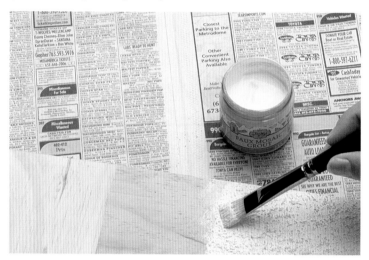

2. Cut six ¼" (6 mm) strips of the pink paper, using the paper trimmer. Cut the strips into 40 to 45 pieces about 1" (2.5 cm) long and 32 to 36 pieces about ⅜" (1 cm) long. Cut four ¾" (2 cm) strips, crosswise, from the striped paper. Cut the strips into 56 to 60 pieces ⅜" (1 cm) long. Cut eight ¼" (6 mm) squares of the brown paper.

3. Cut the rose paper into irregular shapes. As you are cutting the paper, arrange the pieces in order on your work surface. Keep cutting pieces until you have enough to cover the frame.

4. Arrange the paper pieces over the dry grout on the frame, leaving space between the pieces for the grout to show through. Place the brown squares at the eight inner and outer corners. Outline the frame edges with the longer pink pieces; outline the frame opening with the shorter pink pieces. Arrange the rose paper pieces so they fit back together like a puzzle. Plan for 14 or 15 striped pieces along each side of the frame.

5. Adhere the pieces to the frame, one at a time, using the special glue (step 2 of the Faux Mosaic Kit). Apply an even coat, making sure all the edges and corners are glued down. Allow the glue to dry. Check that all the edges are firmly attached. Use a toothpick to apply glue to any loose edges.

6. Apply the faux glaze (step 3 of the Faux Mosaic Kit) to one "tile" at a time. Squeezing the tube gently, first outline the tile with a thin line of glaze. Then fill in the rest of the tile with a thin layer of glaze. Allow the glaze to dry completely. Repeat the glazing process two more times. To glaze the "tiles" along the frame edges, prop the frame on its side between stacks of books. Allow each side to dry before moving to the next side.

DESIGNER'S TIPS

Faux mosaic can be done on a variety of surfaces. The process works nicely on mats as well. It turns a plain picture into an art piece.

◆

Be sure to clean the paintbrush right away with soap and water after applying grout.

Fabric Collage

Self-adhesive fabric layering

An adorable frame is quick and easy to create using self-adhesive fabrics from the craft store. You simply cut the shapes, peel off the paper backing, and apply them to a flat, wood frame. Much like a crazy quilt, there are no rules for where to place the patches. Choose several coordinating fabrics in different prints, including one that has a floral motif large enough to use as an appliqué.

MATERIALS

◆ Wood craft frame

◆ Self-adhesive fabric in a variety of coordinating prints and patterns

◆ Fabric shears or rotary cutter and cutting mat

◆ Metal ruler

◆ Fabric pinking shears

1. Cut four pieces of fabric to cover the four corners of the frame, using the fabric shears or rotary cutter and cutting mat. The size should include the depth of the frame plus about 1" (2.5 cm) to extend onto the frame back. Remove the paper backing from one piece of fabric. Smooth the fabric onto the upper left corner of the frame front, over the left edge, and onto the back. Then wrap the fabric over the top edge and onto the back, folding in the corner as if wrapping a gift. Repeat at the remaining three corners, wrapping the sides first and then the top or bottom edges.

2. Cut pieces of various shapes from two or three different fabrics to fill in the bare areas of the frame front. Cut the pieces with a combination of straight and pinked edges to create a varied look. The pieces along the inner and outer edges should be long enough to cover the edge and extend onto the frame back. Apply the pieces one at a time, overlapping the edges slightly.

3. Cut out two large floral motifs for appliqués. Apply the appliqués over the fabric collage at the sides of the picture opening.

4. Cut out any phrases or small motifs with pinking shears. Apply them randomly around the frame.

5. Insert the picture into the frame.

DESIGNER'S TIPS

You can create your own self-adhesive fabrics by using PeelNStick™ double-sided adhesive. Thin cotton fabrics work the best. Remove the protective paper from one side of the adhesive and smooth the fabric in place. I used a brayer to make this process even easier. After cutting the shapes to size, remove the paper backing from the opposite side to apply the fabric to your frame.

◆

Embellish and personalize your frame with ribbons, beads, or charms.

Bright and Bold

Painted glass

This project makes a modern statement with its simple block forms and bold use of color. The frame itself is an inexpensive document frame that consists of a sheet of glass and a backing board held together with metal clips. The design is painted on the front of the glass with acrylic enamel paints, creating an art "frame" around the photo.

- 11" × 14" (28 × 35.5 cm) frameless frame (glass and backing board held together with metal clips)
- Black spray paint
- Glass cleaner
- Paper towels
- Photograph
- 11" × 14" (28 × 35.5 cm) sheet of graph paper
- Pencil
- Craft acrylic enamel paint: red, fuchsia, bright blue, green, yellow orange, blue green, white, and black
- Plastic or paper plate for mixing paint
- Soft-bristle paintbrushes: 1" (2.5 cm) wash brush and #6 flat, shader
- Water
- Applicator bottle with fine tip

1. Remove the clips that hold the glass to the backing board. Spray the smooth side of the backing board with black paint. Set the backing board aside to dry. Clean the glass thoroughly with glass cleaner and paper towels.

2. On the 11" × 14" (28 × 35.5 cm) sheet of graph paper, draw a rectangle the same size as the photo in the desired location. Mark a grid of 1" (2.5 cm) squares around the rectangle extending three rows out on all sides. Mark the desired color for each square, using the photograph on page 48 as a guide. Place the paper under the glass.

3. Squeeze a quarter-sized dollop of one paint color onto the paper plate. Using the wash brush, paint in the squares of that color with a generous coat. Allow the paint to dry completely. Apply a second coat of the same color to each square, allowing the paint to dry completely.

4. Squeeze a quarter-sized dollop of the first paint color onto the paper plate and add a dime-sized dollop of white

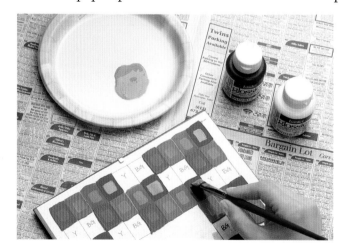

paint. Mix the paints together thoroughly. Using the #6 shader brush, paint a small pastel square in the center of each larger square. Allow to dry. Apply a second coat, if necessary.

5. Repeat steps 3 and 4 for each paint color.

6. Attach the fine metal tip to the applicator bottle. Fill the bottle half full of black enamel paint. Gently squeeze the bottle to get the paint flowing. Outline each 1" (2.5 cm) square and each inner square. Allow the paint to dry completely.

7. Place the glass, painted side up, over the painted side of the backing board, sandwiching the picture between them in the opening. Reattach the metal clips.

DESIGNER'S TIP

Instead of painting the backing board, you can insert a piece of black or colored paper, cut to size, behind the photo. Or, omit painting the backing board of the frame and extend the painted pattern to the edges of the glass.

A Cheery Note

Chalkboard paint and wood beads

Special chalkboard paint transforms this frame into a unique surface for leaving notes. You can make one for each member of the family, so everyone has a personal message board. The chalkboard paint must be "seasoned" as indicated in step 7, if you want to erase messages. I've added playfulness and color with wood beads and mini candle cups, available at craft stores.

MATERIALS

- ✦ Wood craft frame, 10" (25.5 cm) square

- ✦ Sanding sponge and tack cloth, optional

- ✦ Chalkboard spray paint, black

- ✦ Craft acrylic paints: white, bright red, yellow, grape, ultra blue, fuchsia, leaf green, ocean reef blue, and bittersweet orange

- ✦ #10 shader soft-bristle paintbrush

- ✦ 18 unfinished wood mini candle cups, ⅝" (1.5 cm) tall

- ✦ 36 unfinished wood beads, ½" (1.3 cm) diameter

- ✦ Metal ruler

- ✦ White chalk

- ✦ One box 4-d bright finish nails, 1½" (3.8 cm) long

- ✦ Small tack hammer or eyelet hammer

- ✦ Cotton rag

1. Sand the frame smooth, if necessary, using a sanding sponge. Wipe the frame with a tack cloth to remove any dust particles.

2. In a well-ventilated area, spray the frame on both sides with an even coat of chalkboard paint. Allow the paint to dry completely. Apply a second coat, making sure all areas are thoroughly covered.

3. Paint the mini candle cups with white paint, using the shader paintbrush. Apply a second coat if necessary, allowing the paint to dry between coats.

4. Using the other acrylic paints, paint five beads bright red, six beads yellow, four beads grape, four beads ultra blue, five beads fuchsia, four beads leaf green, four beads ocean reef blue, and four beads bittersweet orange. Apply two light coats of paint, allowing the paint to dry between coats.

5. Mark the placement for nine evenly spaced nails on each edge of the frame, using the white chalk and metal ruler. The outer nails should be about ½" (1.3 cm) from the corners of the frame.

6. Using the photo on page 52 as a guide for color arrangement, thread the beads and mini candle cups onto the nails and pound them in gently with a hammer at the marks. Always turn the candle cups so the larger hole faces the frame.

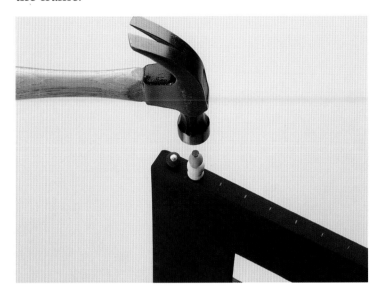

DESIGNER'S TIP

Before painting the beads, thread them on a bamboo skewer. Wrap a piece of tape around the skewer below the last bead to keep them from falling off the skewer. This way you are able to paint all sides of the beads without handling them and getting paint on your hands. You can do the same thing with the mini candle cups. If the holes are too big for one skewer, use two or three skewers.

7. Turn the chalk on its side and rub it over the front of the frame to season the paint. Buff off the chalk with a cotton rag.

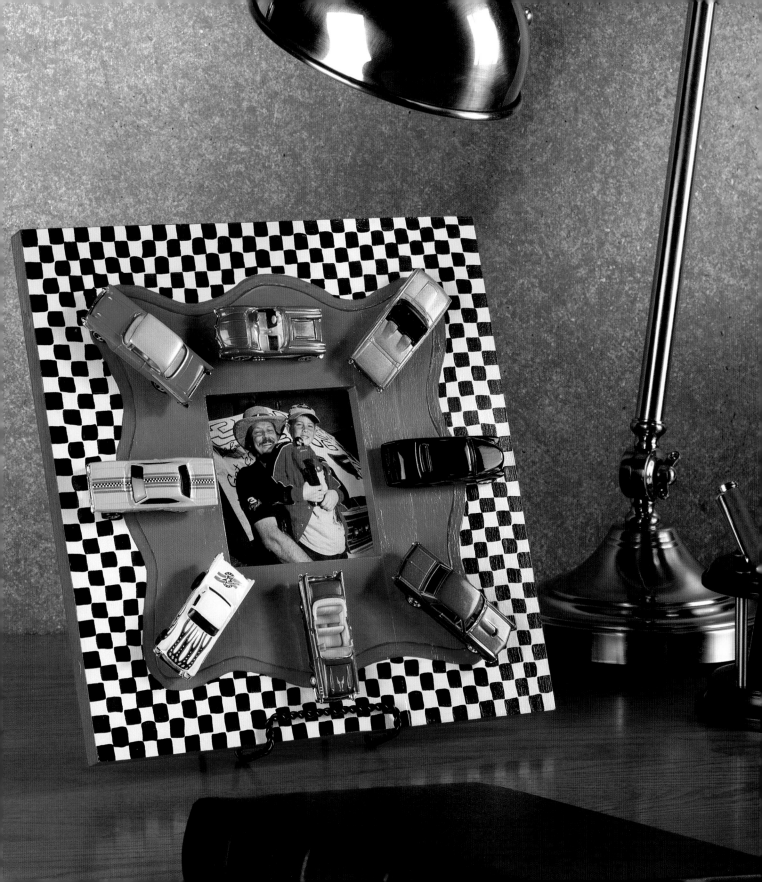

Classic Cars

Decorative painting and collectible toys

Car lovers will enjoy the fun, retro look of this frame. All you need is a plain wood frame, paints and a paintbrush, and toy cars. Frames can be customized for people who love classic cars, extreme cars, racing cars, or whimsical cars just by the toy cars you choose. Shopping for the toy cars to make this frame was half the fun!

- ◆ Wood craft frame, 12" (30.5 cm) square with 4" (10 cm) square opening

- ◆ Sanding sponge and tack cloth, optional

- ◆ Craft acrylic paints: black, white, bright red, and leaf green

- ◆ Soft-bristle paintbrushes: 1" (2.5 cm) wash brush and #6 shader

- ◆ Pencil

- ◆ Gloss acrylic varnish

- ◆ Eight toy cars

- ◆ Hot glue gun and glue sticks

1. Sand the frame smooth, if necessary, using a sanding sponge. Wipe the frame with a tack cloth to remove any dust particles.

2. Using the wash brush, apply two coats of white paint to the entire frame, allowing the paint to dry completely between coats.

3. Mark a free-form scallop-edged square 2" to 2½" (5 to 6.5 cm) from the frame opening, using a pencil. Paint the area inside the scallop-edged square, including the inner edges of the opening, with leaf green paint, using the wash brush. Apply two coats, allowing the paint to dry between coats.

4. Load the #6 shader brush with black paint. Beginning at an outer corner of the frame, paint a square the width of the brush. Leave a brush-width space and paint another square. Continue around the frame edge. Then paint rows of squares in a checkered design up to the green area.

> ### DESIGNER'S TIP
>
> *The same basic design can be adapted for other small collectibles, for example, a miniature china tea set or tiny kitchen utensils.*

5. Load the #6 shader brush with red paint. Paint a border along the edge of the green area the width of the brush. Also paint the sides of the frame red. Apply two to three coats, allowing the paint to dry completely between coats.

6. Using the wash paintbrush, apply two coats of gloss, allowing the varnish to dry completely between coats.

7. Arrange the cars as desired on the frame front. Attach each car to the frame, using a generous amount of hot glue on the underside of the car. For cars with large wheels, place the glue on the inside wheel wells and tires. Insert your photograph into the frame opening.

Pompeii

Faux aged plaster

This deep red frame has the Old World look of aged plaster. The frame can be created in many colors and works in many décor styles. The application is much like the Venetian-plastered walls popular in restaurants and homes but is done on a much smaller scale using dimensional craft paints. This is an easy, forgiving, and fun paint project even for the complete beginner.

MATERIALS

◆ Wood craft frame

◆ Waxed paper

◆ Dimensional paint, 1 to 2 tubes each of country red, raspberry, and sienna

◆ Plastic or metal palette knife

◆ Paper towels, optional

1. Place the frame facedown on a piece of waxed paper. Squeeze a wavy line of country red dimensional paint onto the frame back. Using the palette knife, spread the paint gently in a thin layer, leaving a slightly textured surface, as if you were frosting a cake. Add more paint as necessary to cover the back and sides of the frame and the inner edges of the opening. Allow the paint to dry completely.

2. Turn the frame right side up. Apply the country red dimensional paint to the front, as in step 1, covering the rest of the frame. Allow the paint to dry completely.

3. Squeeze a half-dollar-sized dollop of raspberry dimensional paint onto the waxed paper. Using the palette knife, scoop up a small amount of the paint and smear it onto a small area of the frame, creating an irregular, slightly textured highlight. Repeat as desired over the frame front. Allow the paint to dry completely.

4. Squeeze a quarter-sized dollop of country red dimensional paint, a nickel-sized dollop of raspberry dimensional paint, and a dime-sized dollop of sienna dimensional paint onto the waxed paper. Gently mix the paints together to create a marbled mixture, using the palette knife. Apply the mixture sparsely around the frame in random, short strokes of the palette knife, overlaying some of the country red and raspberry areas. Allow the frame to dry completely.

5. Insert your photograph into the frame opening.

DESIGNER'S TIPS

This frame can be personalized to reflect a Spanish, Southwest adobe, or cowboy look just by changing the color scheme. Simply pick your favorite color, another color one shade lighter, and a brown tint.

♦

Don't be afraid to add texture. Lightly pounce the palette knife on the paint to create ridges and peaks.

♦

If you want a smoother look, wipe the palette knife often with a paper towel.

Wedgwood

Dimensional paint scrolls

Old Wedgwood china, with its characteristic blue color and crisp white raised design, inspired me to create this frame. Though the design may look complicated, it is really quite easy when you break it down into steps, beginning with slender curved lines and gradually adding flourishes and dots. Practice first on a flat surface—it's like decorating a cake! You don't have to hurry, as the paint dries slowly.

MATERIALS

+ Wood craft frame

+ Sanding sponge and tack cloth, optional

+ Soft-bristle wash paint-brush, 1" (2.5 cm) wide

+ Craft acrylic paint, dusty periwinkle blue

+ Small circle decorative applicator tip

+ Two tubes of white dimensional paint

1. Sand the frame smooth, if necessary, using a sanding sponge. Wipe the frame with a tack cloth to remove any dust particles.

2. Using the wash brush, apply two coats of the blue paint to the frame, allowing the paint to dry between coats.

3. Attach the small circle decorative applicator tip to the dimensional paint tube. Apply the paint to the frame front in a series of curved lines that will form the framework of the scroll design. Hold the tip above the frame while squeezing the tube gently and moving it along the desired path.

4. Add extensions and connecting lines to the framework of curved lines.

5. Add pull-dots to the base lines, following the directions at right. You can overlap pull-dots to create a fan at the end of a line or, for additional embellishment, where the lines come together. Add small dots alongside the lines or in open spaces. Allow the dimensional paint to dry completely.

6. Insert your photograph into the frame opening.

Encrusted Glass

Dimensional glass painting and beadwork

Elegant details of a traditional wedding dress are echoed in this ornate frame. The clear glass frame is decorated with scrolls of dimensional paint and accented with crystal and metallic beads. Though the appearance is delicate, the beaded wires are actually very secure. The beads are added to embedded wires only after the paint is dry, so the wires can be manipulated and you won't have to worry about smudging.

- ◆ Document frame
- ◆ Glass cleaner
- ◆ Paper towels
- ◆ Tracing paper, optional
- ◆ Pencil, optional
- ◆ Two tubes silver air-dry dimensional outliner paint
- ◆ One spool tinned copper 24-gauge wire, cut into 80 pieces, 2" (5 cm) long
- ◆ Wire cutter
- ◆ E beads, 160 each of gold and silver
- ◆ 80 clear crystal beads, 6 mm
- ◆ 80 pearl seed beads
- ◆ Needle-nose pliers

1. Clean the frame thoroughly, using glass cleaner and paper towels.

2. Enlarge the pattern (opposite) by 300% and place it underneath the frame.

3. Unscrew the applicator tip from the outliner paint tube, and use the tip to pierce the opening of the paint tube. Attach the applicator tip.

4. Apply the outliner paint to the frame, following the pattern. Gently squeeze the tube from the bottom and keep the applicator tip just above the surface of the glass to form dimensional lines. Working on one design section at a time, apply the framework curves first. Then add the extensions and connecting lines.

5. To add the pull-dots, touch the applicator tip of the paint tube to the glass surface, a short distance from the end or

side of a base line. Squeeze out a plump dot of paint and release the pressure on the tube. Pull the tip back toward the base line, connecting the dot tail to the base line. Because wires will be embedded in the pull-dots, allow an ample buildup of paint at these areas.

6. Allow the paint to dry for 20 minutes. Gently slide a 2" (5 cm) wire into each pull-dot at an angle, embedding ½" (1.3 cm) of the wire into the paint. Apply another pull-dot of paint over each entry point and tail to ensure that the wires are thoroughly embedded. Allow the paint to dry completely without disturbing the wires.

7. Place a gold bead, silver bead, crystal bead, silver bead, gold bead, and seed bead on an exposed wire. Bend the wire end into a tiny curlicue to secure the beads, using the needle-nose pliers. Bend the beaded wire into a gentle arc. Repeat for each wire.

DESIGNER'S TIPS

To keep costs down, you can substitute glass or plastic beads for the crystal beads.

◆

Though the wires will be secure, they will come out if you bend or yank on them too much, so be careful.

◆

To clean the completed frame, blow dust away with a can of spray air. To remove smudges, do not spray the frame directly with glass cleaner as you might damage the paint. Instead, spray a paper towel or cloth with glass cleaner first, and then wipe the center of the frame.

Scroll pattern

Encrusted Glass ◈ 71

A beautiful sunset ends
our day of seashell collecting
on Captiva Island, Fl April 2001

Seashells Shadow Box

Dimensional layering of shells

Gathering shells along the beach is one of my favorite pastimes. After a trip to Captiva Island, I created this shadow-box display. Complete with sand, it is an artistic setting for a beach photo and a shell collection. Shadow boxes allow you to build depth in layers. To attach the seashells, I first glued them to pressed glass marbles, and then glued the marbles in place. The marbles give the shells more stability and allow you to use far less glue.

MATERIALS

- ✦ Shadow box
- ✦ Spray adhesive
- ✦ ⅓ yd. (0.32 m) blue fabric
- ✦ Scissors
- ✦ Foam core board, ½" (1.3 cm) thick
- ✦ Craft knife and cutting mat
- ✦ Metal ruler
- ✦ Photograph
- ✦ Scrap of paper
- ✦ Tape
- ✦ Sand
- ✦ Old spoon or plastic spoon
- ✦ Acid-free adhesive dots
- ✦ Assorted shells, including four small scallops
- ✦ Hot glue gun and glue sticks
- ✦ 1⅛ yd. (1.05 m) sky blue ribbon, ½" (1.3 cm) wide
- ✦ Pressed glass marbles
- ✦ Paper for caption
- ✦ Black fine-tip, acid-free marker
- ✦ Mini-scallop decorative-edge scissors

1. Remove the backing box and glass from the shadow-box frame. Set the glass aside. Spray the inside of the backing box, using spray adhesive. Smooth the fabric in place on the bottom and up the sides of the box. Cut out excess fabric at the corners to allow it to fit smoothly.

2. Cut a piece of foam core board about 4" (10 cm) wider and longer than your photograph, using the craft knife, cutting mat, and metal ruler. Cut the scrap of paper to the size of your photo and tape it in the middle of the foam core board. Spray the foam core board with spray adhesive and sprinkle sand all over the surface, using a spoon. Tap off any excess sand.

3. Remove the scrap paper. Adhere the photograph to the foam core board, using acid-free adhesive dots. Using the hot glue gun, attach the four small scallop shells at the corners of the photograph to look like photo holders. Using a small amount of hot glue, attach the ribbon around the foam core edge.

4. Using the hot glue gun, attach nine pressed marbles, round side down, to the back of the foam core board in three rows of three. Glue the flat side of the marbles to the bottom of the frame box in the desired location.

5. Arrange the remaining shells in small clusters in the shadow box and glue them in place. To give a shell more stability and a better gluing surface, glue a pressed marble inside the shell, flat side out. Then glue the marble in place.

6. Using the acid-free marker, write a caption for your photo on a small piece of paper. Cut the caption out with mini-scallop decorative-edge scissors. Curl the strip of paper around the marker to make it wavy. Using a small amount of hot glue, attach the caption to the frame.

7. Reassemble the shadow box.

It Was a Very Good Year

Framed wine corks

A memory box presentation is an original way to create meaningful artwork from memorabilia. This frame was designed to hold corks that a couple saved from special dinners during their courtship. Sophisticated script art paper comes in a sheet large enough to cover the entire mat board in one piece. The velvet fabric over the backing board and the velvet and satin medallions at the corners of the ribbon border create a grand setting for the corks.

1. Remove the backing board, mat, and glass from the shadow box. Spray the backing board with spray adhesive. Adhere the red velvet, and smooth it into place. Cut excess fabric even with the edge of the backing board.

2. Place the mat over the backing board as a guide. Arrange the wine corks in three rows of three. Attach the corks to the backing board one at a time, using the hot glue gun.

3. Place the art paper facedown on the cutting mat; center the frame mat facedown over the paper. Trace the mat opening and mark an X from corner to corner. Cut on the X, using the craft knife, cutting mat, and metal ruler, creating four flaps. Cut the flaps to 1" (2.5 cm).

4. Remove the mat. Spray the back of the script art paper, using spray adhesive. Place the mat back over the paper, aligning the opening to the marked lines; smooth paper into place. Fold the short flaps over the edges of the opening to the mat back, creating a nicely finished edge.

5. Cut four pieces of black grosgrain ribbon, each 2½" (6.5 cm) longer than the sides of the mat opening. Using a small amount of hot glue, attach the ribbons to the front of the mat, ¼" (6 mm) from the opening edges, forming a border.

6. Cut the black satin ribbon and red velvet ribbon into four 12" (30.5 cm) pieces. Using a needle and thread, run a basting stitch along one long edge of one ribbon. Pull the thread to gather the ribbon, forming a tight circle. Knot the thread, and hand-stitch the short ends of the ribbon together. Repeat for each ribbon.

7. Cut four 1" (2.5 cm) circles from the gold paper, using mini zigzag decorative-edge scissors. Using sharp-tip scissors, cut slits into the edges of the circles, creating fringe. Punch a small hole in the center of each gold circle and place a decorative brad through the hole. Layer the red ribbon circle on top of the black ribbon circle. Place the fringed gold circle and decorative brad on top. Secure the decorative brad to hold the ribbon medallion together.

8. Attach a ribbon medallion at each corner of the ribbon border, using the hot glue gun. Place the frame facedown. Reassemble the shadow box, inserting the mat first, followed by the glass, and then the backing board.

DESIGNER'S TIP

You can personalize this frame to hold silver baby rattles, a pocket watch, or any other elegant mementos.

Beaded Quartet

Grouping of embellished mini frames

Jeweled and embellished frames are popular, and can be pretty pricey, too. You can create the look with inexpensive mini frames, wire, and beads. This shadow box is a creative way to show off a quartet of beaded mini frames, often sold as place card holders. Bead the frames to look the same or different. This posh look works equally well for vintage photographs or contemporary snapshots.

MATERIALS

- ✦ Shadow box
- ✦ Four silver place card holder frames
- ✦ 24-gauge tinned copper wire
- ✦ Beads of your choice; I used 6 mm colored glass beads, 4 mm beads, metallic pony beads, mini pony beads, and disk beads
- ✦ Wire cutter
- ✦ Needle-nose pliers
- ✦ Tape
- ✦ Hot glue gun and glue sticks

1. Remove the backing board from each of the four place card holder frames. Remove the stands from the backings and discard. Set the backing boards aside.

2. Prepare beaded wires in various styles for decorating the frames. For best results, prepare the same number, style, and bead sequence for all corners and for opposite sides of each frame.

SINGLE BRANCH: Cut a piece of wire 2" to 3" (5 to 7.5 cm) long, using the wire cutter. Thread a bead onto the center of the wire, and fold the wire in half. Twist the wire two or three times just under the bead. Thread other beads onto both wire tails to the desired length. Wrap tape over the ends of the wire to hold the beads temporarily.

SPLIT BRANCH (WORKS WELL FOR CORNERS): Cut a piece of wire 3" to 4" (7.5 to 10 cm) long, using the wire cutter. Thread a bead onto the center of the wire, and fold the wire in half. Twist the wire two or three times just under the bead. Thread two beads onto both wire tails. Separate the wires and string the desired number of beads onto each wire in matching sequences. Wrap a piece of tape over the ends of the wire to hold the beads temporarily.

ARCHED BRANCHES: Cut a piece of wire about ½" (1.3 cm) longer than the desired finished length, using the wire cutter. Wrap one end of the wire with tape. Thread the desired beads onto the wire. Wrap the other wire end with tape just beyond the last bead.

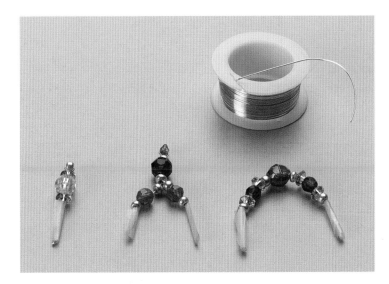

DESIGNER'S TIPS

For this project, some of the wires must be twisted tightly to secure the beads. Use needle-nose pliers for a cleaner and more polished look. Needle-nose pliers help curl the end of a wire to secure beads in place. They can also crimp, hold things in place, and help you get a tighter grip on the wire than with your bare fingers.

◆

For a more uniform appearance, use the same style of beading around each of the mini frames.

3. Remove the tape, and secure the beaded wires to the frame back, one at a time, using the hot glue gun. Hold the wire ends in place until the glue hardens.

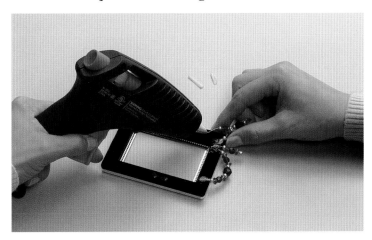

4. Arrange the beaded frames on the backing board of the shadow box as you desire. Using the hot glue gun, secure the mini frames to the backing board. Reassemble the shadow box.

Garden Fairies

Whimsical floral decorations

You can turn a shadow box into a fantasy garden for a special photograph. Grass and flowers surround the image. The fairies are artist's manikins with flowing dresses of flower petals and netting. Sponge-painted clouds float through a blue sky on the backing board. Wouldn't this lovely frame be the perfect accent for a special little ballerina's bedroom?

MATERIALS

- White shadow box
- Craft acrylic paint: light blue and white
- Soft-bristle wash brush
- Makeup sponge; paper towels
- Foam core board, ½" (1.3 cm) thick
- Craft knife and cutting mat
- Metal ruler
- Green spray paint
- One bag of green excelsior
- Hot glue gun and glue sticks
- Scissors
- Eight packages each of pink and cream hydrangea blossoms
- 30 silver mini brads
- Acid-free adhesive dots
- 1 yd. (0.92 m) pink velvet ribbon, ⅝" (15 mm) wide
- 10 yd. (9.15 m) roll of tulle ribbon, 6" (15 cm) wide
- Two wood art manikins, 4" (10 cm) tall
- Dental floss
- Three stems of velvet leaves
- One silk rose
- 2 yd. (1.85 m) pink ribbon, ⅜" (9 mm) wide
- Small ribbon roses, 10 each of pink and white
- Two artificial branches

1. Remove the backing board from the frame. Using the wash brush, paint the backing board with two coats of light blue paint. Allow the paint to dry completely between coats.

2. Dip the small makeup sponge into the white paint; dab excess paint onto a paper towel. Lightly sponge clouds in a random pattern onto the backing board, and allow it to dry.

3. Cut a piece of foam core board 2" (5 cm) longer and wider than the photograph you wish to mount, using the craft knife, cutting mat, and metal ruler. Spray the foam core frame with the green spray paint and allow it to dry.

4. Mark a 2" (5 cm) border on the green foam core frame. Secure green excelsior to the border, using the hot glue gun. Trim any stray pieces of excelsior, using scissors.

5. Open seven packages of hydrangea blossoms. Layer a small blossom over a large blossom and secure with a silver mini brad. Repeat to make 12 to 15 sets. Insert mini brads through the rest of the single blossoms. Arrange the flowers in groups on two opposite corners of the foam core frame. Attach the flowers, using hot glue.

6. Mount the picture on the foam core frame, using acid-free adhesive dots. Using a small amount of hot glue, attach the pink velvet ribbon to the edge of the frame.

7. Dress each fairy: Cut six 20" (51 cm) pieces of tulle. Accordion-fold each piece into 4" (10 cm) layers. Tie each tightly at the center, using dental floss. Hot glue three tulle tufts to each fairy, just below the waist—one at center front and the others on the back of each hip—creating a full skirt. Arrange the tulle to fill gaps.

8. Hot-glue a large velvet leaf over the tulle on each side of her waist. Cut a small velvet leaf in half and glue the pieces over her shoulders to create little cap sleeves. Cut one medium leaf in half lengthwise and glue one half to each fairy around the bodice.

9. Separate the petals of the silk rose. Glue a layer of overlapping petals at the waist, forming the top layer of the skirt. Layer hydrangea blossoms above the skirt to form the bodice.

10. Cut a 10" (25.5 cm) piece of pink ribbon. Wrap the fairy's waist twice and tie a bow on the back with the ribbon tails hanging off each side. Cut an 18" (46 cm) piece of ribbon. Make a four-loop bow with 1½" (3.8 cm) loops. Glue the bow to the center of the fairy's back to form wings. Glue alternating pink and white ribbon roses around the fairy's head to form a wreath.

11. Attach the backing board to the frame. Break the artificial branches into smaller pieces, if necessary. Glue the branches in opposite corners of the shadow box, using hot glue, allowing them to trail out over the frame. Glue the flower frame in place on top of the branches. Glue the fairies into place opposite the blossom corners, and pose them as if they were flying.

Garden Fairies 87

Fun Floral Art

Silk flowers and dimensional paint

Framing isn't just for pictures! You can add a punch of color to a wall with a simple shadow box, paint, and bright silk flowers. There are lots of choices in the silk floral department of a craft store. Dots of dimensional paint, applied straight from the tube, create a lattice look on the mat board. This project is a fun accent for a bathroom, sun porch, or child's room. For even more impact, make a set with a different flower in each frame.

- ◆ Square shadow box with mat
- ◆ Craft acrylic paints: leaf green and white
- ◆ Soft-bristle paintbrush, 1" (2.5 cm) wide
- ◆ Metal ruler
- ◆ Pencil
- ◆ Small circle decorative applicator tip
- ◆ Dimensional paint, white
- ◆ Silk flowers to fit opening of frame
- ◆ Wire cutter
- ◆ Hot glue gun and glue sticks

1. Remove the backing board, mat, and glass from the shadow box. Save the glass for another craft project, as it is not needed for this project.

2. Using the wash brush, paint the mat with two coats of leaf green paint, allowing the paint to dry completely between coats.

3. Paint the frame with three coats of white paint, allowing the paint to dry completely between coats.

4. Lightly mark a diamond pattern on the mat, using a ruler and pencil.

5. Attach the small circle decorative applicator tip to the dimensional paint tube. Squeeze continuous rows of tiny dots along the marked lines on the mat. To create the perfect dot, touch the applicator tip to the mat, squeeze,

release, and pull the tube up. If you make a mistake, wait until the dimensional paint dries and then lightly peel it off. Allow the dimensional paint to dry completely.

6. Place the mat back into the frame and attach the backing board.

7. Cut the stems of the silk flowers to ¼" (6 mm), using a wire cutter. Discard the cut stems.

8. Determine how the flowers will be arranged in the frame opening. Attach the stems to the backing board with ample amounts of hot glue.

DESIGNER'S TIPS

For this frame, I used six carnations in two columns of three. You may need more or fewer flowers, depending on how they fit the opening in the frame. Take the frame to the store with you.

◆

Practice the method for making tiny paint dots on a scrap of cardboard before applying the dots to the mat.

Place Setting

Framing unexpected items

Many interesting objects around your home can become artwork for your walls. When my husband and I got married, we received only one place setting of our exquisite silverware pattern. Rather than return it, I mounted it in an elegant frame and hung it on my dining room wall. A foam core backing board covered with velvet set a regal stage for the silver pieces and allowed me to attach them with needle and thread.

MATERIALS

- ◆ 12" (30.5 cm) square scrapbooking frame
- ◆ Foam core board, ¼" (6 mm) thick
- ◆ Craft knife and cutting mat
- ◆ Metal ruler
- ◆ Spray adhesive
- ◆ ⅓ yd. (0.32 m) black velvet
- ◆ Scissors
- ◆ One sheet of green Florentine art paper
- ◆ Bone folder
- ◆ Tape
- ◆ Pinking decorative-edge scissors
- ◆ Hot glue gun and glue sticks
- ◆ 2 yd. (1.85 m) red velvet ribbon, ⅜" (9 mm) wide
- ◆ Four decorative brads in antique pewter finish
- ◆ Set of nice silverware
- ◆ Long straight pins
- ◆ Needle and gray thread

1. Open the frame back. Remove the glass, spacer, and interior papers. The glass is not needed for this project.

2. Cut a piece of foam core board to fit the inside of the frame, using the craft knife, cutting mat, and metal ruler. Spray the foam core board with adhesive. Adhere the black velvet, and smooth it into place. Cut excess fabric even with the edge of the foam core board.

3. Cut the Florentine art paper into strips 2" (5 cm) wide. Fold each strip into ⅜" (1 cm) knife pleats, using a bone folder to ensure crisp pleats. Join strips inconspicuously as needed to make four 12" (30.5 cm) border pieces. Secure the pleats with tape on the back. Trim one edge of each strip with pinking decorative-edge scissors.

4. Secure the pleated paper strips around the edge of the velvet-covered board, using a small amount of hot glue. Cut the overlapping pleated pieces in the corners at 45-degree angles to create a mitered look. Cut four red velvet ribbon pieces the lengths of the sides of the velvet board. Glue the ribbon to the paper strips ½" (1.3 cm) from the pinked edges, crossing the ribbons at the corners. In the center of each ribbon intersection, cut a tiny slit through the ribbon, paper, and foam core board. Push a decorative brad into the slit.

5. Arrange your silverware on the velvet board. Determine locations on each piece where stitches should be made to hold the piece in place, such as just below the spoon bowl, at the base of the fork tines, or on a narrow place of the knife handle. Poke long straight pins into the board on either side of the pieces at these locations. Remove the silverware and push the pins completely through the board.

6. Thread a needle with a double thread and tie the ends together in a good-sized knot. Turn the board on edge and sew the silverware in place, one piece at a time, taking several stitches through the pin holes and tightly around the silverware. After each piece of silverware is attached, tie a secure knot on the back of the foam core board.

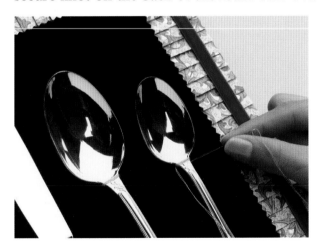

7. Reassemble the frame.

Giverny

Photo transfer with sheer overlay

There are many ways to create attractive artwork from your photographs. For this project, I transferred my photo of Monet's home at Giverny onto fabric using a color copier. The textured silk fabrics and velvet ribbons set off the colors in the photo. To give the image a dreamy appearance, I overlayed it with wide, sheer ribbon.

There are several ways to transfer photos to fabric, using your own computer or the services of a copy shop.

+ Frame with mat

+ ⅓ yd. (0.32 m) green silk dupioni

+ Iron and ironing board, optional

+ Spray adhesive

+ Fabric scissors

+ ¼ yd. (0.25 m) pink silk dupioni

+ Fabric pinking scissors

+ Photo transfer products

+ Clear fabric glue

+ 7" (18 cm) white organdy ribbon, 4" (10 cm) wide

+ 1 yd. (0.92 m) green velvet ribbon, ⅝" (15 mm) wide

+ Metal ruler

1. Remove the backing board from the frame. Press the silk dupioni to remove any wrinkles. Spray the backing board with adhesive. Adhere the dupioni, and smooth it into place. Cut excess fabric even with the edge of the backing board.

2. Cut a piece of pink silk dupioni that is 2¼" (6 cm) wider and longer than your photograph, using fabric pinking scissors. Adhere the pink silk piece in the middle of the green silk piece, using spray adhesive and smoothing it into place.

3. Transfer your photograph onto fabric, following the manufacturer's directions. Or, take your photo to a copy shop to be transferred onto fabric.

4. Glue the photo transfer in the middle of the pink silk piece, using clear fabric glue.

5. Cut a piece of white organdy ribbon ½" (1.3 cm) longer than your photo transfer and place it over the top of the image. Secure the corners, using dots of fabric glue.

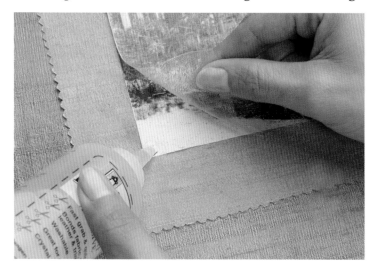

6. Cut four pieces of green velvet ribbon 2" (5 cm) longer than the sides of the pink silk, two of each size. Cut a V-notch in each end of each ribbon. Center a ribbon over each side of the photo, overlapping the edges of the sheer ribbon; secure with dots of glue. Center the remaining ribbons over the top and bottom of the photo, overlapping the cut ends of the sheer ribbon; secure with dots of glue.

DESIGNER'S TIP

If your photograph is wider than 4" (10 cm), you can create the same dreamy effect using sheer silk organdy fabric.

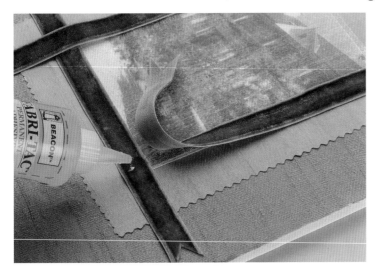

French Memo Board

Changeable photo display

Here is an interesting way to present a collection of photographs. You can change the photos often, or create a permanent presentation. Mount the pictures on colorful acid-free papers or a white acid-free mat for a formal look. The pictures slide in and out under the ribbons. To make an elegant memo board that matches my décor, I bought a plain memo board and covered it with silk fabric and new ribbons.

- ✦ Inexpensive French memo board
- ✦ 1¼ yd. (1.15 m) silk dupioni, color of your choice
- ✦ Iron and ironing board, optional
- ✦ Fabric scissors
- ✦ Staple gun and staples
- ✦ 5 yd. (4.6 m) seam binding or grosgrain ribbon, ⅝" (15 mm) wide, color of your choice
- ✦ Covered-button kit with ¾" (2 cm) buttons
- ✦ Wire cutter
- ✦ Hot glue gun and glue sticks

1. Remove and discard the buttons and ribbons from the original French memo board.

2. Press the silk dupioni to remove any wrinkles, if necessary. Lay the silk facedown on a flat surface; lay the memo board facedown over the fabric. Cut excess silk so there is 2½" (6.5 cm) extra fabric on each side of the memo board. Starting with the long sides, wrap the silk to the back of the board, stretching the fabric taut. Using the staple gun, secure one staple at the center of each side. Repeat on the short sides of the memo board.

3. Wrap the silk over diagonally at each corner, and secure with a staple. Then neatly fold in the remaining fabric and staple in place. Finish stapling the fabric around the memo board.

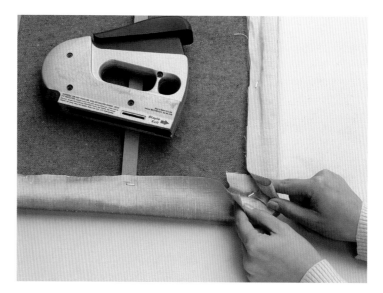

4. Turn the memo board faceup. Cut two ribbon pieces a few inches longer than the distance from corner to corner diagonally. Wrap one end to the back, and staple in place. Stretch the ribbon taut to the opposite corner, wrap the end to the back, and staple. Repeat with the second ribbon, forming an X. Add four more ribbons parallel to the first ones, stretching them taut from the mid-points of each side.

5. Insert a staple at each ribbon intersection. Using scraps of silk dupioni, make five covered buttons, following the manufacturer's directions. Remove the button shanks, using the wire cutter. Using the hot glue gun, attach the buttons, hiding the staples at each ribbon intersection.

Circled in Satin

Ribbon wreath

A wreath of ribbons makes this frame burst with energy, personality, color, and texture! The wreath is made by tying satin ribbons to a wire wreath frame. The circular mat is cut with a special tool designed to cut circles of any diameter accurately and quickly. If you don't have one, ask your local framing shop to cut the mat for you.

MATERIALS

- ◆ 14" (35.5 cm) square frame
- ◆ Wire wreath frame, 12" (30.5 cm) in diameter
- ◆ Wire cutter
- ◆ 3 yd. (2.75 m) each of double-faced satin ribbon, 1" (25 mm) wide, in eight to ten bright colors
- ◆ 3 yd. (2.75 m) each of double-faced satin ribbon, ⅝" (15 mm) wide, in eight to ten colors
- ◆ 2 yd. (1.85 m) double-faced satin ribbon, ⅜" (9 mm) wide, in desired color
- ◆ Fabric shears
- ◆ Acid-free white mat board to fit frame
- ◆ Circle cutter
- ◆ Pencil
- ◆ Hot glue gun and glue sticks

1. Remove the outer ring of the wire wreath frame, using the wire cutter, and leaving the inner three rings intact.

2. Cut all the 1" (25 mm) and ⅝" (15 mm) ribbons into 8" (20.5 cm) pieces. Cut a V-notch in each end of each ribbon. Cut the ⅜" (9 mm) ribbons into 6" (15 cm) pieces. Cut an angle in each end of each ribbon.

3. Tie the ribbons to the wires of the wreath frame. For each piece, fold the ribbon in half beneath the wire. Bring the loop and tails up and insert both tails through the loop above the wire. Pull the tails tight, and spread them apart. Repeat, alternating the colors and widths of ribbon. Fill the outer ring first, the middle ring second, and the inner ring last. Tie the narrow ribbons on the frame crossbars.

4. Mark the center on the back of the mat board. Using the mark as the center point for the circle cutter, cut a hole large enough for your photo. Open the back of the frame. Insert the circular mat and the photograph. Reassemble the frame.

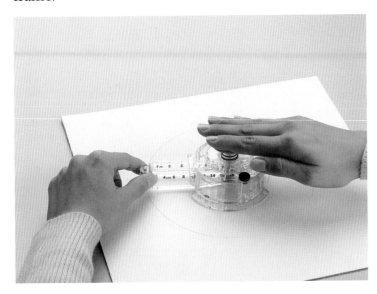

5. Center the ribbon-wrapped wire frame over the photo. Secure it to the glass, using the hot glue gun.

Wild Cards

Playing cards as art

Even playing cards can be art–especially to someone who loves card games, from bridge to poker. This project is perfect for the wall of a game room or den. The special double scrapbooking frame allows extra room for the stacked cards.

+ 12" × 24" (30.5 × 61 cm) frame

+ Spray adhesive

+ One sheet of red and gold pineapple damask art paper

+ Scissors

+ One sheet of white and gold harlequin art paper

+ Craft knife and cutting mat

+ Metal ruler

+ Pinking decorative-edge scissors

+ Deck of playing cards

+ Hot glue gun and glue sticks

1. Remove the backing board from the frame. Spray the backing board with spray adhesive, and smooth the red and gold pineapple damask art paper over it. Cut excess paper even with the edge of the backing board.

2. Cut a 9" × 20" (23 × 51 cm) rectangle of white and gold harlequin art paper, using the craft knife, cutting mat, and ruler. Trim the edges with pinking decorative-edge scissors. Apply spray adhesive to the back of the paper, and smooth the paper in place in the center of the pine-apple damask paper-covered backing board.

3. Separate the cards into individual suits. Fan out two black suits for the left and right side of the backing board. Fan out one red suit in the middle of the board. Secure each fan by gluing the individual cards together, using the hot glue gun. Glue the completed fans to the harlequin paper. Create three fans of face cards, two red suits and one black suit. Glue the cards together. Glue the fans in place, overlapping the first fans.

4. Place a few extra loose cards around the frame randomly. Glue the cards in place. Trim excess cards that hang over even with the backing board, using the craft knife, cutting mat and metal ruler. Reassemble the frame.

DESIGNER'S TIP

Here's a colorful and fun idea for a child's bedroom or playroom—use decks of cards from Go Fish, Crazy Eights, Old Maid, and similar card games.

Sources

Look for the products used in this book at scrapbooking, art, craft, and fabric stores. The manufacturers listed can refer you to a retail or on-line source, and some can sell to you directly.

Simple Elegance
frame: K & Company, LLC; papers: Anna Griffin, Inc. (AG186, AG185, AG174, AG167, and AG164); paper trimmer and scissors: Fiskars Brands, Inc.

Dressed in Pink
frame: Walnut Hollow; scrapbooking papers: Cosmopolitan Scrapbooking Papers by Making Memories; decorative-edge scissors, paper trimmer, circle cutter, and micro tip scissors: Fiskars Brands, Inc.; decorative brads: Decorative Brads Antique Copper Variety Pack 2 by Making Memories

Love Songs
calligraphy pen: Speedball® Art Products Co.

Vintage Paris
papers: by Cavellini, purchased at Paper Zone; Florentine paper by Flax Art & Design; scissors and paper crimper: Fiskars Brands, Inc.; decorative brads: Making Memories; gold paint pen: ZIG® Painty® by EK Success, Ltd.; decoupage medium: Rubber Stampede® Decoupage Medium by Delta Technical Coatings

Victorian Roses and Butterflies
frame: K & Company, LLC; adhesives: 3M™ Super 77™ Spray Adhesive and Scotch® Double-Coated Tape by 3M Corp.; papers and die cuts: Anna Griffin, Inc. (AG180, AG186, AG197, and AG098), cream roses die cuts (AG538), and red butterfly die cuts; scissors and paper trimmer: Fiskars Brands, Inc.; adhesive dots: 3-D Dots™ by EK Success, Ltd.

Springtime Garden
frame and papers: K & Company, LLC; spray adhesive: 3M™ Super 77™ Spray Adhesive; decorative-edge scissors and regular scissors: Fiskars Brands, Inc.; adhesive dots: 3-D Dots™ by EK Success, Ltd.

Military Honors
frame: K & Company, LLC; art paper: Canson; spray adhesive: 3M™ Super 77™ Spray Adhesive; scissors, paper crimper, and stylus: Fiskars Brands, Inc.; adhesive dots: Glue Dots International; decorative brads: Making Memories

Paper Roses
Faux Mosaic Kit™ by Ranger Industries; papers: Flora Bella Collection Cabbage Rose Paper (633186) by K & Company, LLC, Plain Pink (AG015) and Plain Tobacco Brown (AG029) papers by Anna Griffin, Inc.; scissors: Micro-Tip Scissors by Fiskars Brands, Inc.

Fabric Collage
frame: Jen's Frame by Provo Craft; self-adhesive fabric: FabriCraft™ Peel'n'Stick Fabric by Delta Technical Coatings; fabric scissors and pinking scissors: Fiskars Brands, Inc.; double-sided adhesive: PeelNStick™ by Therm O Web

Bright and Bold
paint: Glossies Enamel Paints by Liquitex

A Cheery Note
frame: Walnut Hollow; paint: Chalk Board spray paint by Rust-Oleum® Brands; Ceramcoat® Acrylic Paints by Delta Technical Coatings; wood beads and mini candle cups: Westrim Crafts

Classic Cars
frame: Jen's Frame by Provo Craft; paint: Ceramcoat® Acrylic Paints by Delta Technical Coatings; toy cars: Matchbox and Hot Wheels

Pompeii
frame: Jen's Frame by Provo Craft; paint: Texture Magic™ Dimensional Paint™ by Delta Technical Coatings

Wedgwood
frame: Jen's Frame by Provo Craft; paint and decorative tip: Ceramcoat® Periwinkle Blue Acrylic Paint, Texture Magic™ Dimensional Paint™ and Easy-Twist Detail Tips™ by Delta Technical Coatings

Encrusted Glass
paint: Cernes Relief air-dry outliner by Pebeo; tinned copper wire by Artistic Wire, Ltd.

Seashells Shadow Box
ribbon: Midori, Inc.; scissors: Fiskars Brands, Inc.; adhesive: 3M™ Super 77™ Spray Adhesive

It Was a Very Good Year
scissors: Fiskars Brands, Inc.; paper: Ornate Script Paper Set by Flax Art & Design; ribbon: Midori, Inc.; decorative brads: Making Memories

Beaded Quartet
place card holder frames: Wilton Industries; wire: Artistic Wire, Ltd.

Garden Fairies
spray paint: Design Master; ribbon: Midori, Inc.; blossoms: Making Memories; art manikins: Loew-Cornell

Fun Floral Art
paint and decorative tip: Ceramcoat® Acrylic Paint in Leaf Green and White, Texture Magic™ Dimensional Paint™ and Easy-Twist Detail Tips™ by Delta Technical Coatings

Place Setting
frame: K & Company, LLC; adhesive and tape: 3M™ Super 77™ Spray Adhesive and Scotch® tape by 3M Corp.; paper: Florentine art paper by Flax Art & Design; ribbon: Midori, Inc.; scissors: Fiskars Brands, Inc.; decorative brads: Making Memories

Giverny
photo transfer paper: Lazertran; ribbon: Midori, Inc.; adhesive: 3M™ Super 77™ Spray Adhesive; fabric glue: Fabri-Tac™ by Beacon Adhesives Co., Inc.

French Memo Board
staple gun and staples: Black & Decker; scissors: Fiskars Brands, Inc.; seam-binding ribbon: Midori, Inc.; covered button kit: Prym Dritz

Circled in Satin
frame: K & Company, LLC; ribbon: Midori, Inc.; circle cutter: Fiskars Brands, Inc.

Wild Cards
art papers: Midori, Inc.; scissors: Fiskars Brands, Inc.; adhesive: 3M™ Super 77™ Spray Adhesive

Manufacturers

3M Corp.
888-364-3577
www.3m.com

Anna Griffin, Inc.
888-817-8170
www.annagriffin.com

Artistic Wire, Ltd.
630-530-7567
www.artisticwire.com

Beacon Adhesives Co., Inc.
800-865-7238
www.beaconcreates.com

Black & Decker
www.blackanddecker.com

Canson
www.canson.com

Delta Technical Coatings/Rubber Stampede®
800-423-4135
www.deltacrafts.com

Design Master
303-443-5214
www.dmcolor.com

EK Success, Ltd.
800-524-1349
www.eksuccess.com

Fiskars Brands, Inc.
800-950-0203
www.fiskars.com

Flax Art & Design
800-343-3529
www.flaxart.com

Glue Dots International
www.gluedots.com

Hot Wheels
www.hotwheels.com

K & Company, LLC
888-244-2083
www.kandcompany.com

Lazertran
800-245-7547
www.lazertran.com

Liquitex
888-422-7954
www.liquitex.com

Loew-Cornell
201-836-7070
www.loew-cornell.com

Making Memories
800-286-5263
www.makingmemories.com

Matchbox
www.matchbox.com

Midori, Inc.
800-659-3049
www.midoriribbon.com

Paper Zone
206-467-1028
www.paperzone.com

Pebeo
www.pebeo.com

Provo Craft
800-937-7686
www.provocraft.com

Prym Dritz
www.dritz.com

Ranger Industries
800-244-2211
www.rangerink.com

Rust-Oleum® Brands
800-323-3584
www.rustoleum.com

Speedball® Art Products Co.
800-898-7224
www.speedballart.com

Therm O Web
800-323-0799
www.thermoweb.com

Walnut Hollow
800-950-5105
www.walnuthollow.com

Westrim Crafts
www.westrimcrafts.com

Wilton Industries
800-794-5866
www.wilton.com